THI

Skinny INDIAN
TAKEAWAY

RECIPE BOOK

THE SECRET TO LOW CALORIE INDIAN TAKEAWAY FOOD AT HOME. BRITISH INDIAN RESTAURANT DISHES UNDER 300, 400 & 500 CALORIES

The Skinny Indian Takeaway Recipe Book
The Secret To Low Calorie Indian Takeaway Food At Home. Authentic British Indian Restaurant dishes under 300, 400 & 500 Calories

A Bell & Mackenzie Publication
First published in 2013 by Bell & Mackenzie Publishing
Copyright © Bell & Mackenzie Publishing 2013

ISBN 978-0-9576447-7-9

Disclaimer
The information and advice in this book is intended as a guide only. Any individual should independently seek the advice of a health professional before embarking on a diet. Some recipes may contain nuts or traces of nuts. Those suffering from any allergies associated with nuts should avoid any recipes containing nuts or nut based oils.

Contents

Contents

Contents

THE
Skinny INDIAN
TAKEAWAY
RECIPE BOOK

INTRODUCTION

Introduction

Indian takeaway curry has never been more popular (or more fattening!). We all love the taste of takeaway and there are times when simply nothing else will do. Whether you enjoy a quiet Korma or a roaring Rogan Josh, The Skinny Indian Takeaway Recipe Book lets you in on the secret of making real takeaway meals without the gut-busting calories.

If you're trying to watch your weight, blowing all your hard work with a Friday night curry puts you back to square one, but what's the alternative? A supermarket bought 'light' curry?......No Thanks! Tasteless and tiny is not what you're after when you crave a takeaway. That's why we have developed the Skinny Indian Takeaway Recipe Book so that you can still enjoy your favourite takeaway without piling on the pounds or compromising on the taste. So EASY even a BEGINNER can master these authentic recipes in minutes – just like your favourite dish from your local restaurant.

 ## What This Book Will Do For You

The Skinny Indian Takeaway Recipe Book will teach you to cook the UK's best loved British Indian Restaurant Style meals in minutes, in your own home and at a fraction of the cost and calories. Plus we'll be revealing the secret behind the classic takeaway curry taste and how we make it SKINNY!

How We Do It

Like most takeaway curries our recipes rely on a secret curry base mix which forms the basis of almost all the curries you'll ever eat. Think of it as the foundation from which every curry begins and creates that authentic takeaway taste. The difference is we have developed a special SKINNY curry base mix which loses lots of the calories but none of the taste. We've followed that through with each individual recipe and by carefully choosing alternative low fat ingredients it's now possible to enjoy a real Chicken Tikka Masala or Lamb Rogan Josh without ruining your diet.

Cooking Made Simple

It's easy to be overwhelmed by the idea of Indian cooking. With the cuisine relying so heavily on spice blends you can be put off by the vast array on offer before you've even started. Don't be afraid of spices - you'll get to know them quickly and become confident in your cooking in no time. The Skinny Indian Takeaway Recipe Book demystifies Indian cooking by using just a handful of key spices which you can use time and time again throughout the book and which, once bought, you can keep in the store cupboard for ages and go back to month after month saving you money in the long run.

Plus our SKINNY curry base mix can be made in advance and frozen in batches so that you can put a tasty curry together in superfast time whenever you fancy it.

History of British Curry

Curries have become an integral part of British cuisine. Its real popularity began in Britain during the 19th and early 20th centuries with Britain & India's close connections through the British Raj. The first curry house is believed to have opened in London in 1810 and for 150 years curry houses were predominately run by Bengali people. British Indian food differs significantly from traditional Indian cuisine with dishes often sharing a name but being pointedly different in taste and ingredients.

British style curry has become a cuisine of it's own and British Indian Restaurants are now popular in their own right in America, Canada, Australia and New Zealand.

 ## What You Should Know

Although many characteristics of British Curry are shared commonly across restaurants, often individual restaurants will have their own spin on even the most well known dishes and can therefore vary dramatically - not everyone's Tikka Masala is the same! In this book we have tried to cover the most common dishes and the ways in which they are prepared. To make them exactly like your local takeaway you might need to experiment a bit. For example if your 'local' puts green beans in their Lamb Rogan Josh or whole almonds in their Chicken Korma then feel free to copy to get your authentic 'postcode' taste.

To keep things Skinny we have used low fat or low calorie ingredients where possible. If you want to make any of the dishes richer substitute some of the ingredients for the higher fat alternatives and use more oil, but bear in mind this will impact the calorie count.

Serving Sizes

Most of the dishes in this book serve 2. You can alter the quantities to serve more if you like, however don't just double the quantities. If for example you decide to cook for 4, double the meat and sauce/liquid quantities but only increase the spices, salt and sugar by 50%.

Calories & Measurements

The calories stated on each menu are the recipe ingredients only, anything you add to this will obviously increase the calories.

- Unless stated, calories for each meat dish have been based on 300g skinless chicken breasts. Other meats may increase calories.
- Also feel free to substitute vegetables for meat if that's what you prefer, this will bring your calorie count down even more.
- Adding salt, sugar and spice heat to your meals is a question of taste. Feel free to adjust the recipes to suit your own preferences.
- Teaspoons and tablespoon measurements in the recipes are heaped.

Cooking Tips

Getting the consistency of your curry right is key to the takeaway experience. If you feel like it's not thick enough leave to cook for a little longer with the lid off to thicken the sauce. Likewise if it's too thick add some water to loosen things up during cooking.

Also make sure your spices don't burn, this is really important. As we've really cut down on the oil to make the meals skinny you might find adding a drop of water to the pan when you are cooking the dry spices helps. Final thing to mention is the use of sugar.
If you find any of your curries have a slight bitterness to them add some sugar to counteract, use small amounts each time to make sure you don't over do it.

The main thing is to be confident, get started and you'll be cooking delicious takeaway style curries in no time.

THE

Skinny INDIAN
TAKEAWAY

RECIPE BOOK

HERBS
& SPICES

Herbs & Spices – A Rough Guide

Using herbs and spices in cooking is something we take for granted now around the world but it wasn't always that way. The story of the trading between historic civilizations in Asia, Northeast Africa and Europe is a drama which encompasses wars, revolutions, bloodshed, slavery and greed which is both shocking and fascinating. Once spices were widely tasted things would never be the same again and their use has fused cultures and food for many millennia!

There are literally hundreds of herbs and spices which can be used to flavour and enhance Indian cuisine. What follows is a list of the main ones used in this book along with a brief description to give you a understanding of their role in a dish.

Cardoman seeds
Green cardoman is one of the world's most expensive spices with a unique aromatic taste which should be used sparingly. This book uses Cardoman seeds which is a cheaper alternative.

Chilli Powder
Chilli powder is often a mix of different types of chilli which have been dried and pulverised to create a chilli blend. It is used to add pungency to cooking and can be bought in various differing strengths.

Ground Cinnamon
Gathered from the bark of Cinnamomum trees, cinnamon is used in both sweet and savoury dishes and adds an aromatic sweetness to cooking.

Ground Coriander
Also known as Chinese parsley or cilantro, coriander is often one of the spices in the spice blend garam masala. The ground version is used in this book but fresh leaves are a lovely garnish you could add.

Ground Cumin
Harvested from a flowering plant which is part of the parsley family, cumin is an absolute must in a great deal of Indian cuisine. The use of cumin seeds and ground cumin is common and adds an earthiness and warmth to the meal.

Curry Powder
Basically a 'shortcut' ingredient, British curry powder generally contains a mix of coriander, turmeric, cumin, ginger & garlic. Most UK versions have a pleasant but fairly generic taste.

Fennel Seeds
Fennel is a highly aromatic and flavourful herb which can taste a little like aniseed. Fennel seeds are often eaten raw in India as a breath freshener and eye sight improver!

Fenugreek Seeds
Fenugreek has a distinctive sweet smell which is unmistakable. The seeds are oddly shaped diamonds which are often roasted and used extensively in Indian cooking.

Garam Masala
The original 'curry powder' garam masala is a blend of spices which usually includes peppercorns, coriander, cloves, cinnamon, cumin seeds & cardamom pods amongst others.

Garlic Powder
Simply ground dehydrated garlic cloves. Easy to grow and cultivate all year round Garlic has been used in cooking for thousands of years and adds a lovely depth to Indian cuisine.

Ground Ginger
Cooking ginger has a warm aromatic smell which, once you know it, is recognisable in any restaurant or kitchen.

Paprika
Paprika is made from ground chillies and/or peppers. It is often used to add colour as well as flavour & pungency to dishes.

Saffron
The bitter taste and fragile 'angel hair' strands of Saffron have been traded and fought over for more than four thousand years. It is one of the world's most expensive spices and is more valuable per Kg than gold!

Turmeric
Native to tropical South Asia turmeric adds colour to cooking. It's bright yellow/orange appearance has the ability to stain almost anything it touches and should be handled with care. It is an absolute basic staple of Indian cooking and smells delicious and truly 'Indian'.

THE SECRET

Skinny Curry Base Mix
Makes 12 Servings

Ingredients:

1 tbsp sunflower oil
1 large onion chopped
2 carrots, sliced
1 tsp garlic powder
1 tsp cumin
1 tsp turmeric
1 tsp paprika
½ tsp garam masala
1 tsp ground coriander

½ tsp ground ginger
1 tsp salt
1 tsp sugar
2 tbsp tomato puree
1 400g/14oz can chopped tomatoes
600ml/2 ½ cups boiling water with 1 chicken stock cube

Method:

1 Gently sauté the onions and carrots in the oil for a few minutes.
2 Add all the dried spices and tomato puree and cook for another minute or two.
3 Add the stock, salt, sugar and chopped tomatoes, cover and leave to simmer very gently for 40 minutes.
4 Blend until completely smooth and split into portions. You can keep chilled for a few days or freeze for a few months.

This skinny curry base sauce will form the base of most of the curries you make. You can divide or multiply the quantities to suit you. It makes sense to make up quite a big batch so you have it to hand when you fancy making a curry.

THE

Skinny **INDIAN**
TAKEAWAY

RECIPE BOOK

CURRIES

Bhuna
Serves 2

427 CALORIES PER SERVING

Ingredients:

2 portions skinny curry base mix
300g/11oz lean meat, cubed
100g/3 ½ oz chopped vegetables
2 onions chopped
¼ tsp cardamom seeds
½ fenugreek seeds and ground ginger
1 tsp ground garlic
1 large tomato chopped

½ red or green pepper sliced
½ tsp each turmeric, chilli powder, ground coriander, cumin & garam masala
1 tbsp low fat natural yoghurt
1 tbsp tomato puree
½ tbsp lemon juice
½ tsp salt
1 tsp sugar
2 tsp sunflower oil

Method:

1 Brown the meat in 1 tsp of sunflower oil, add the chopped tomato and pepper
for 2 minutes of further cooking and move to one side.
2 Mix the turmeric, chilli powder, garam masala, coriander, cumin in a cup with a little water to form a paste. Add another tsp of oil into the frying pan and turn the heat to medium.
3 Add the spice mix, cardamom and fenugreek seeds stirring constantly for 20 seconds. Add the sugar, onion, ginger and garlic and gently cook for a few minutes before adding the tomato puree.
4 Next add the meat back into the pan along with the skinny curry base mix and cook for 20 minutes or until your meat is tender and properly cooked through. Stir through the yoghurt and lemon and serve.

Bhuna is a medium curry with a thick sauce which usually contains vegetables. Use whatever you have to hand but a mix of carrots, cauliflower and peas is a good place to start.

Butter Chicken
Serves 2

Ingredients:

2 portions skinny curry base mix
300g/11oz cooked chicken tikka pieces (see page 42 for preparation instructions)
15g/ ½oz butter
½ tsp sugar

½ tsp salt
½ tsp each of garlic powder, garam masala, coriander, chilli powder & ground ginger
2 tbsp tomato puree
1 tbsp lemon juice
60ml/ ¼ cup single cream

Method:

Gently warm your skinny curry base mix through in a pan. Meanwhile heat the butter in a frying pan and add the meat tikka pieces (see page 42 for preparation instructions), ground spices & tomato puree and cook through. Add the warmed curry base sauce, sugar and salt to your meat mixture and stir well. Leave to heat thoroughly until piping hot. Take off the heat, stir through the cream and serve straight away.

Butter Chicken is a beautiful creamy dish which is usually enormously calorific. This skinny version comes out at under 500 calories without losing the smoothness or taste.

Dopiaza
Serves 2

397
CALORIES
PER SERVING

Ingredients:

2 portions skinny curry base mix
300g/11oz lean meat
1 tsp each garlic powder, cumin, coriander, fenugreek seeds, chilli powder, curry power, garam masala

1 tsp sugar
2 large onions cut into half moon slices
½ tsp salt
2 tsp sunflower oil

Method:

Brown the meat in the frying pan with 1 tsp sunflower oil for a few minutes. Put the meat on a plate to one side and gently fry the onions in the same frying pan with another teaspoon oil. Cook until tender and then add the meat, spices, sugar and salt and combine well. Add the skinny curry base mix, cover and cook for 20 minutes or until the meat is tender and cooked through.

Dopiaza or Dupiaza means double onions. The use of onions and a thick sauce characterise this dish.

Jalfrezi
Serves 2

Ingredients:

2 portions skinny curry base mix
300g/11oz lean meat cubed
1 medium onion thinly sliced
2 tsp sunflower oil
½ tsp each garlic powder, ground ginger, cumin, coriander & turmeric
1 red pepper sliced
1 tsp sugar
½ tsp salt
4 green chillies sliced
1 tsp chilli powder
4 fresh tomatoes, chopped
1 tbsp tomato puree

Method:

Heat 1 tsp sunflower oil a frying pan. Add the meat and brown on a medium/high heat for a few minutes. Place on a plate to one side.

In the same pan add the rest of the oil and gently fry the onion, pepper and chilies for a few minutes until soft. Combine the dry spices in a cup with a little water and add to the pan with the tomato puree, continue frying for 2 mins. Add the skinny curry base mix to the pan and warm for a minute or two.

Next add the chopped tomatoes and browned meat to the pan and simmer for 20-25 mins or until the meat is tender and properly cooked through

Jalfrezi should always contain green chillies and onions. It recently usurped Chicken Tikka Masala in a national poll as the UK's most popular curry dish.

23

Garlic Chicken
Serves 2

407
CALORIES
PER SERVING

Ingredients:

2 servings skinny curry base mix
300g/11oz lean meat, cubed
8 garlic cloves, peeled and very thinly sliced
2 tsp sunflower oil
1 tsp garlic powder
1 tsp ground ginger

1 tsp cumin
1 tsp mild chilli powder
1 tsp mild curry power
1 tbsp tomato puree
2 fresh tomatoes chopped
½ tsp salt
1 tsp sugar

Method:

Brown the meat in a frying pan with 1 tsp of sunflower oil. Set the meat to one side and gently fry the garlic in the same pan using the other tsp of sunflower oil. After a minute or two of gentle frying stir in the dry spices and tomato puree. Return the meat to the pan along with the salt, sugar, fresh tomatoes and skinny curry base mix. Cover and leave to simmer for 20 mins or until the meat is tender and cooked through.

Garlic Chicken is sometimes called Garlic Chilli Chicken. To make this spicier, if you prefer, introduce chopped fresh chillies.

Korma
Serves 2

Ingredients:

2 portions skinny curry base mix
300g/11oz lean meat cubed
1 tsp mild curry powder
¼ tsp ground ginger
½ tsp ground garlic, turmeric, garam masala, cumin
1 bay leaf

60ml/ ¼ cup low fat coconut milk
½ tsp sugar
½ tsp salt
Few drops natural yellow food colouring
2 tsp sunflower oil

Method:

Add the sunflower oil to a frying pan and brown your meat on a medium/high heat. Meanwhile mix the dry spices in a cup with a little water to make a smooth paste. Turn the meat to a low heat, add the spice paste, sugar, bay leaf and skinny curry base mix. Stir well and leave to simmer for approx 20 minutes or until the meat is properly cooked through.
Finally add the coconut milk and food colouring, warm through gently and serve.

A mild, yellow curry, Korma usually contains almonds and/or coconut. This skinny version uses low fat coconut milk.

Madras
Serves 2

418 CALORIES PER SERVING

Ingredients:

2 portions skinny curry base mix
300g/11oz Lean meat
2 small onions finely chopped
1 tsp medium curry powder
½ tsp each of turmeric, fenugreek seeds, coriander, garlic powder, ground ginger, paprika & garam masala

3 fresh tomatoes chopped
1 tbsp tomato puree
1 ½ tsp chilli powder
½ tsp crushed cardamom seeds
½ tsp salt
1 tsp sugar
2 tsps lemon juice
2 tsp sunflower oil

Method:

Add 1 tsp of sunflower oil to a frying pan on a medium heat, brown the meat for a few minutes then place to one side.

Mix the dry spices in a cup with a little water to form a paste. Using the same pan add another teaspoon of sunflower oil, the onions, the spice mix liquid and lemon juice. Cook on a gentle heat until the onions are softened.

Next introduce the skinny curry base mix, mixing all ingredients thoroughly then add your browned meat, tomatoes and tomato puree.

Cover, simmer and cook for 20 minutes or until the meat is tender and cooked through.

Known as the standard hot curry in the UK. Madras has a fiery reputation.

27

Rogan Josh
Serves 2

Ingredients:

2 portions skinny curry base mix
300g/11oz lean cubed meat
1 tsp each garlic powder, ground ginger, cumin powder, garam masala
1 tsp sugar
½ tsp turmeric powder & ground cinnamon

2 tbsp ground almonds
2 tsp curry powder
1 tbsp paprika
½ tsp ground cinnamon
Pinch ground cloves
2 tbsp low fat greek yoghurt
1 tbsp tomato puree
3 chopped tomatoes
½ tsp salt

Method:

Brown the meat in the frying pan with 1 tsp sunflower oil. Add all the dry spices to a cup with a little water, create a paste and add to the meat pan, continue to cook gently. Add the tomato puree and chopped tomatoes and cook for a further minute before adding the skinny curry base mix and ground almonds. Cover and continue to simmer for 20 minutes or until the meat is tender and cooked through. Stir through the yoghurt just before serving.

Rogan Josh is an aromatic dish of Persian origin popular in the Kashmir region.

Tandoori Chicken
Serves 2

Ingredients:

6 chicken drumsticks
1 tsp sunflower oil
3 tbsp lemon juice
1 tsp chilli powder
1 tsp salt
250ml/1 cup low fat greek yoghurt

1 tsp each of garlic powder, turmeric & garam masala
½ tsp cumin, black pepper, ground ginger & paprika
Couple of drops red food colouring

Method:

Puncture the drumsticks with a skewer or knife to make lots of little holes in the flesh. Add the oil, lemon juice, chilli powder and salt to the chicken and rub in really well. Place in the fridge for a couple of hours. Meanwhile mix together all the other ingredients and smother the drumsticks with this mixture. Leave in the fridge overnight.

Put the drumsticks on a wire rack over a baking tray and cook in a pre-heated oven at 200C/400F/Gas Mark 6 for 30-40 minutes or until the meat is properly cooked through.

This skinny version of Tandoori chicken gets the marinade to do all the work turning regular chicken drumsticks into authentic takeaway tandoori chicken.

Tandoori King Prawn Masala

485 CALORIES PER SERVING

Serves 2

Tandoori Ingredients:

500g/1lb 2oz raw king prawns
1 tsp sunflower oil
3 tbsp lemon juice
1 tsp chilli powder
1 tsp salt
120ml/ ½ cup low fat greek yoghurt
1 tsp each of garlic powder, turmeric & garam masala
½ tsp cumin, black pepper, ground ginger & paprika
Couple of drops red food colouring

Masala Ingredients:

2 portions skinny curry base mix
1 tsp sugar
½ tsp salt
1 tsp sunflower oil
½ tsp each of garlic powder, chilli powder & ground ginger
1 tsp medium curry powder
1 tsp garam masala
2 tbsp tomato puree
2 tbsp low fat greek yoghurt

Method:

Add the oil, lemon juice, chilli powder and salt to the prawns and rub in really well. Place in the fridge for a couple of hours. Meanwhile mix together all the other Tandoori ingredients and smother the chilled prawns with this mixture. Leave in the fridge overnight.

Put the prawns on a wire rack over a baking tray and cook in a pre-heated oven at 200C/400F/Gas Mark 6 for 10 minutes or until they are properly cooked through.

Warm your skinny curry base mix through in a pan. Gently heat the sunflower oil in a frying pan and add the cooked Tikka prawns, ground spices, tomato puree, skinny curry base mix, sugar and salt to your prawn mixture and stir well. When piping hot take off the heat, stir through the yoghurt and serve immediately.

Marinated tandoori prawns form the basis of this lovely masala which is often listed as a chef's special recipe in UK restaurants and takeaways.

Tikka Masala
Serves 2

402 CALORIES PER SERVING

Ingredients:

2 portions skinny curry base mix
300g/11oz Tikka Pieces (see page 42 for preparation instructions)
1 tsp sugar
½ tsp salt
1 tsp sunflower oil

½ tsp each of garlic powder, mild chilli powder & ground ginger
1 tsp mild curry powder
2 tbsp tomato puree
3 drops natural red food colouring
2 tbsp low fat greek yoghurt

Method:

Gently warm the skinny curry base mix through in a pan. Meanwhile heat the oil in a frying pan and add the meat tikka pieces (see page 42 for preparation instructions), ground spices & tomato puree and cook through. Add the warmed curry base sauce, sugar and salt to the meat mixture and stir well. Leave to heat through thoroughly until piping hot. Take off the heat, add the yoghurt and red food colouring to the mixture, stir well and serve straight away.

The classic British curry!
Adopted as the UK's national dish, Chicken Tikka Masala is one of the all time most popular British curries; although in recent years it has relinquished it's top-dog crown to Jalfrezi.

Traditional Curry
Serves 2

Ingredients:

300g/11oz Lean meat diced
2 portions skinny curry base mix
2 tsp mild curry powder
½ tsp salt
1 tsp sugar

2 tbsp tomato puree
½ tsp each ground garlic, cumin, coriander, paprika & turmeric powder
120ml/ ½ cup single cream
1 tsp sunflower oil

Method:

Brown the meat in a frying pan with the sunflower oil. Add the dried spices, curry powder and tomato puree and gently cook for a minute or two. Add the skinny curry base mix, sugar & salt and leave to cook for 20 minutes or until the meat is tender and completely cooked through. Take off the heat, stir through the cream and serve.

This simple 'medium' curry differs greatly from restaurant to restaurant. The Skinny version here is finished off with a generous measure of single cream.

Dhansak
Serves 2

380 CALORIES PER SERVING

Ingredients:

1 portion skinny curry base mix
300g/11oz lean meat, cubed
1 tsp tomato puree
1 tbsp curry powder
½ tsp ground garlic
½ tsp ground ginger
½ tsp turmeric

½ tsp garam masala
½ tsp chilli powder
½ tsp salt
1 tsp sugar
100g/3 ½ oz pineapple chunks
& 1 tbsp pineapple juice
2 tsps sunflower oil

Method:

Brown the meat in a frying pan with 1 tsp sunflower oil. Add all the dry spices and tomato puree and cook for a further 2 minutes. Stir in the skinny curry base mix, cover and leave to cook gently for approx 20 minutes or until the meat is tender and cooked through. Add the pineapple chunks and juice and warm through. Serve immediately.

Dhansak is usually cooked with chicken or beef and includes pineapple and pineapple juice.

Vindaloo
Serves 2

Ingredients:

2 portions skinny curry base mix
300g/11oz lean meat
2 tsp hot chilli powder (or to your taste)
1 tbsp white wine vinegar
1 tsp each - turmeric, paprika, garlic, cumin, garam masala

1 onion sliced
1 tbsp tomato puree
1 tsp sugar
½ tsp salt
2 tsp sunflower oil

Method:

Seal the meat in a frying pan with the sunflower oil. Add the dry spices and vinegar and cook for a few minutes. Add the tomato puree, salt, sugar and skinny curry base mix and stir well. Cover and leave to cook for 20 minutes or until the meat is tender and cooked through.

Vindaloo is all about the heat! The version here is reasonably hot but feel free to adjust to your taste.

Chicken & Garlic Chaat

Serves 2

320 CALORIES PER SERVING

Ingredients:

300g/11oz chicken breast cubed
2 tsp sunflower oil
½ tsp salt

4 cloves garlic crushed
1 tsp ground coriander, turmeric and mild chilli powder
2 tbsp lemon juice

Method:

Add the oil to a pan and stir fry the chicken pieces for 5-6 minutes. Add the salt, garlic, coriander, turmeric and chilli powder and gently cook for a few minutes or until the chicken is completely cooked through. Remove from the heat and stir in the lemon juice. Serve with a green salad.

Chaat is the term to describe savoury food which is typically served as street food in Pakistan and India. This simple chicken dish is delicious fast food which is also often served as a starter.

Biryani
Serves 2

461 CALORIES PER SERVING

Curry Ingredients:

150g/5oz lean meat, diced
2 portions skinny curry base
mix
2 tsp mild curry powder
½ tsp salt
1 tsp sugar
2 tbsp tomato puree
50g/2oz frozen peas
½ tsp each ground garlic,
cumin, coriander, paprika &
turmeric powder
120ml/ ½ cup single cream
1 tsp sunflower oil

Rice Ingredients:

100g/3 ½oz basmati rice
½ onion, finely chopped
¼ tsp ground cinnamon
¼ tsp ground cloves
1 bay leaf
Pinch of Saffron
1 chicken stock cube
1 tsp sunflower oil

Method:

Brown the meat in a frying pan with the sunflower oil. Add the
dried spices, curry powder and tomato puree and gently cook for
a minute or two. Add the skinny curry base mix, peas, sugar & salt
and leave to cook for 20 minutes or until the meat is tender and
completely cooked through.
Meanwhile cook the rice.
Rinse the rice really well in a sieve with cold water.
Boil a pan of water and dissolve a cube of chicken stock into it.
Meanwhile gently fry the onion, cinnamon and cloves for a few
minutes. Add the rice to the onion mix and coat, transfer contents
of frying pan plus the bay leaf and saffron into the boiling stock
water and cook until tender.
When both the rice and curry are ready take off the heat and stir
the cream through the curry. Combine the rice and curry together
to make a takeaway style biryani.

This version of the classic spiced rice and sauce dish
prepares both elements separately before combining right
at the end.

Phall
Serves 2

Ingredients:

2 portions skinny curry base mix
300g/11oz lean meat
2 tsp hot chilli powder
2 scotch bonnet chillies, seeds removed finely chopped
1 tbsp white wine vinegar
1 tsp turmeric, paprika, garlic, cumin

½ tsp ginger, garam masala, fennel seeds
1 onion sliced
200g/7oz chopped tomatoes
2 tbsp tomato puree
1 tsp sugar
½ tsp salt
2 tsp sunflower oil

Method:

Seal the meat in a frying pan with the sunflower oil. Add the dry spices, chillies and vinegar and cook for a few minutes. Add the tomato puree, tomatoes, salt, sugar and skinny curry base mix and stir well. Cover and leave to cook for 20 minutes or until the meat is tender and cooked through.

Phall is a purely British invention. It developed as a dish in the UK's Indian restaurants when customers repeatedly asked for something hotter than a vindaloo.

39

Prawn Puri
Serves 2

Ingredients:

400g/14oz small cooked peeled
prawns
2 tsp sunflower oil
2 onions chopped
4 tomatoes chopped
½ red pepper chopped

100g/3 ½oz frozen peas
1 tsp cumin, garam masala &
coriander
1 teaspoon ground cumin
2 tbsp lime juice
½ tsp salt

Method:

Heat the oil in the pan and gently fry the onion. After a few
minutes add the tomatoes, red pepper and peas and leave to cook
for about 5 minutes more until the tomatoes starts to lose their
shape. Add the salt, spices and prawns and cook until the prawns
are piping hot. Remove from the heat and stir through the lime
juice. Serve with chapati bread.

*Puri bread is a skinny problem so the serving
suggestion is chapati bread which works just fine with
this recipe, which is also often served as a starter.*

Pasanda
Serves 2

Ingredients:

2 portions skinny curry base mix
300g/11oz lean cubed meat
1 tsp each chilli powder. garlic powder, ground ginger, cumin powder, garam masala & curry powder

1 tsp sugar
½ tsp turmeric powder
4 tbsp ground almonds
4 tbsp low fat greek yoghurt
½ tsp salt
Handful chopped coriander and almonds to garnish

Method:

Brown the meat in the frying pan with 1 tsp sunflower oil. Add all the dry spices to a cup with a little water to create a paste. Add to the meat pan and continue to cook gently. Add the skinny curry base mix, sugar, salt and ground almonds. Cover and continue to simmer for 20 minutes or until the meat is tender and cooked through. Stir through the yoghurt just before serving.

Ground almonds usually characterise this dish but cashew nuts and/or coconut milk can also be used.

Skinny **INDIAN**
TAKEAWAY

RECIPE BOOK

STARTERS &
SIDE DISHES

Chicken or Lamb Tikka

Serves 2

Ingredients:

300g/11oz lean meat, cubed
120ml/ ½ cup low fat natural yoghurt
1 tsp turmeric ground cumin, garam masala, coriander, mild chilli powder, garlic powder

½ tsp ground ginger
1 tbsp lemon juice
Pinch salt
2 drops red food colouring

Method:

Mix all the spices, food colouring and lemon juice together to form a paste. Add the yoghurt and mix through.

Combine the meat into the mixture and leave to marinade in the fridge overnight.

Put the meat pieces on a wire rack over a baking tray and cook in a pre-heated oven at 200C/400F/Gas Mark 6 for 8-10 minutes. Turn each piece over and put back in the oven for a further 8-10 minutes or until the meat is properly cooked through.

You can eat the Tikka hot or cold skewered on a wooden kebab stick with salad to serve, or freeze for use in other dishes which require Tikka pieces.

Tikka forms the basis of a number of curries including Tikka Masala and Butter Chicken. It is also delicious as a standalone starter with salad and Cucumber Raita.

45

Sheik Kebab
Serves 2

Ingredients:

150g/5oz lean lamb mince
½ tsp ground coriander, garlic, salt
½ onion very finely chopped
1 green chilli very finely chopped

1 tsp shop bought mint sauce
1 tsp lemon juice
1 tsp sunflower oil
Wooden skewers

Method:

Leave 4 wooden skewers to soak in water for a few hours.
Gently fry together the onion, green chillies, coriander and garlic for a few minutes.
Place the lamb, lemon juice, mint sauce and warm spicy onions into a food processor and whizz together until well mixed. Take the mixture out and place on a chopping board. Divide into 4 portions and roll into sausage shapes around each skewer. Grill under a medium heat for 12-15 minutes or until the lamb is properly cooked through.
Serve with a side salad and yoghurt dip.

Lean mincemeat and light spices make this a lovely starter which is best served with a plain salad.

Shami Tikka
Serves 2

Ingredients:

150g/5oz lean lamb mince
½ tsp ground coriander, garlic,
salt, paprika, cumin & turmeric
1 green chilli very finely
chopped

1 tbsp freshly chopped mint
1 tsp lemon juice
1 tsp sunflower oil
½ onion very finely chopped

Method:

Gently fry together the onion, green chillies, coriander, paprika, cumin, turmeric and garlic for a few minutes.

Place the lamb, lemon juice, chopped mint and warm spicy onions into a food processor and whizz together until well mixed. Take the mixture out and place on a chopping board. Divide into 8 portions and shape into small flat meat patties. Grill under a medium heat for 10-12 minutes or until the lamb is properly cooked through.

Serve with a side salad and yoghurt dip.

Shami Tikka differs from Sheik Kebab with its flat patties and inclusion of paprika, turmeric and cumin.

Bombay Potatoes
Serves 2

Ingredients:

1 tbsp sunflower oil
¼ tsp mustard seeds
1 tsp mild chilli powder
½ tsp turmeric powder

200g/7oz potatoes, boiled and
cubed
½ tsp salt

Method:

Mix the chilli and turmeric in a cup with a little water to form a paste.

Heat the oil in a pan. When it is hot add the mustard seeds and cook for a minute or two until they start to pop. Add the spice paste to the mustard seeds along with the boiled cubed potatoes and cook for a few minutes until the potatoes are completely covered in the spice mix and piping hot.

Bombay potatoes are one of the simplest and most popular of all Indian side dishes.

Saag Aloo
Serves 2

219 CALORIES PER SERVING

Ingredients:

1 portion skinny curry base Mix
60ml/ ¼ cup low fat coconut milk
½ onion chopped
500g/1lb 2oz baby spinach leaves

1 green chilli chopped
100g/3 ½ oz potatoes, cubed
1 tsp mild curry powder
1 tsp sunflower oil
½ tsp each salt & sugar

Method:

Gently fry the onion and green chilli in the sunflower oil for a few minutes. Add the potatoes and curry powder, fry for a minute longer then add the skinny curry sauce mix, spinach, salt & pepper. Cover and leave to simmer gently until the potatoes are tender. Remove from heat, stir through the coconut milk and serve.

Saag Aloo is the general term for leafed dish. In the UK spinach is most often the leaf used, however mustard leaves or finely chopped broccoli can also be substituted.

Aloo Gobi
Serves 2

290 CALORIES PER SERVING

Ingredients:

1 cauliflower head split into florets
1 400g/14oz can chopped tomatoes
1 tbsp sunflower oil
1 onion chopped
Handful of shredded green cabbage
200g/7oz peeled diced potatoes

Handful chopped coriander
1 tsp chilli powder
½ tsp garlic powder
½ tsp ground ginger
1 tsp sugar
1 tsp cumin
2 tsp turmeric
1 tsp garam masala
1 tsp salt

Method:

Add the oil and onions into a frying pan and gently cook. Mix in the dried herbs, salt and fresh coriander and cook for a further minute or two. Next add the sugar, cabbage, chopped tomatoes, cauliflower and potatoes, cover and cook on the lowest possible setting for at least 20 minutes. Make sure the vegetables are completely tender before serving.

Aloo Gobi is a chance for the much-maligned cauliflower to shine in this spiced, dry, vegetable side dish.

Minted Lamb
Serves 2

Ingredients:

150g/5oz lean cubed lamb meat
2 tbsp balsamic vinegar
½ tsp garam masala
½ tsp turmeric
½ tsp garlic

½ tsp coriander
½ tsp salt
1 red onion, chopped
1 tsp shop bought mint sauce
1 tbsp sunflower oil
120ml/ ½ cup boiling water

Method:

Brown the lamb off in a frying pan with the sunflower oil on a high heat. Remove the lamb and very gently fry the onions for a few minutes. Combine the spices and vinegar with the cooking onions, return the meat to the pan and mix well. Add the mixture to an oven proof dish with the mint sauce and boiling water. Cover and cook in a preheated oven at 180C/350F/Gas5 for an hour or until the meat is tender and the water has reduced down.

Cubed lean meat, light spices and slow cooking make this a tasty tender starter which is lovely served with chapatti to dip in the juices.

53

Mixed Vegetable Curry

215 CALORIES PER SERVING

Serves 2

Ingredients:

1 portion skinny curry base mix
100g/3 ½ oz frozen peas
1 carrot, peeled & cut into batons
1 onion, chopped
Handful chopped spinach
½ head cauliflower broken into florets

50g/2oz potatos, cubed
1 tsp sunflower oil
1 tbsp tomato puree
½ tsp cumin, turmeric & coriander
1 tsp mild curry powder
1 tsp mild chilli powder
½ tsp salt

Method:

Heat the sunflower oil in a pan and gently fry the onion. After a few minutes add the other vegetables and continue to cook. Mix the dry spices in a little water and add to the pan along with the salt and skinny curry base. Cover and leave to cook gently until all the vegetables are tender.

Using only 1 portion of Skinny curry base mix keeps this versatile dish reasonably dry and structured in shape.

THE

Skinny INDIAN
TAKEAWAY

RECIPE BOOK

CONDIMENTS

Poppadoms & All The Extras

Poppadoms, mango chutney, lime pickle, onion salad & mint yoghurt are all synonymous with takeaway curry. There is however is no easy quick way to replicate the first three at home so we recommend shop bought poppadoms, mango chutney & lime pickle. Poppadoms can be particularly high in calories but one way around this is to buy uncooked poppadoms which are suitable for cooking in the microwave rather than fat fryer.

Mint Yoghurt
Serves 2

Ingredients:

250ml/1 cup low fat Greek yoghurt
1 tbsp shop bought mint sauce
Large handful chopped coriander

½ tsp caster sugar (add more or less to your taste)
Salt & pepper

Method:

Combine all the ingredients together. The caster sugar, salt & pepper should be altered to suit your own taste. Cover and chill in the fridge

This is a simple dip which is often served with starters and/or poppadoms.

Cucumber Raita
Serves 2

Ingredients:

¼ peeled cucumber
250ml/1 cup low fat Greek yoghurt
1 spring onion finely chopped

¼ tsp ground cumin
Pinch Cayenne pepper
Salt & Pepper

Method:

Slice the cucumber very thinly and sprinkle with a little salt. Leave for half an hour or more in a bowl as the salt drains some of the moisture from the cucumber. Dry the cucumber slices off and combine with the yoghurt, spring onion and cumin. Adjust the seasoning and sprinkle with a little cayenne pepper. Cover and put in the fridge to chill.

The coolness of the cucumber and yoghurt in this condiment is intended to counteract the heat of particularly fiery curries.

Onion Salad
Serves 2

Ingredients:

1 large mild onion, chopped
¼ cucumber, diced
1 tbsp lemon juice
3 ripe tomatoes, chopped
Handful chopped fresh coriander

Handful chopped fresh mint leaves
Pinch of Salt, black pepper & sugar – adjust these to your taste

Method:

Combine all the ingredients together, adjusting the seasoning and sugar to suit your taste. Cover and chill in the fridge.

The crunch of the onions and sharpness of the lemon are perfect with fresh mint and coriander in this simple accompaniment.

THE
Skinny INDIAN
TAKEAWAY
RECIPE BOOK

BREAD

Chapati
Serves 10

Ingredients:

125g/4oz whole wheat flour
125g/4oz plain flour
1 tsp salt

2 tbsp olive oil
175ml/ ¾ cup hot water

Method:

Stir together both the flours, salt, olive oil and enough of the water to make a soft, not sticky, dough. Knead the dough on a floured surface and divide into 10 balls. Leave for 20 minutes covered. Roll each ball out into a flat 'pancake'.

Heat a frying pan with a spray of 1-cal cooking oil. When the pan is nice and hot put the chapatti on it and cook for 30 secs. Flip and cook for 30 seconds longer.

Indian flatbreads are the perfect accompaniment to almost any Indian dish.

Vegetable Chapati
Serves 10

Ingredients:

125g/4 oz whole wheat flour
125g/4 oz plain flour
1 tsp salt
2 tbsp olive oil
½ head broccoli

½ onion
1 clove garlic
1 green chilli
175ml/ ¾ cup hot water

Method:

Whizz the broccoli, onion and garlic in a food processor to make the smallest pieces possible. Stir together both the flours, salt, olive oil and enough of the water to make a soft, not sticky, dough. Add the vegetable mix and knead the dough on a floured surface and divide into 10 balls. Leave for 20 minutes covered. Roll each ball out into a flat 'pancake'
Heat a frying pan with a spray of 1-cal cooking oil. When the pan is nice and hot put the chapatti on it and cook for 40 secs. Flip and cook for 40 seconds longer.

This vegetable version of the Indian flatbread packs a little kick with the inclusion of green chillies

Spiced Roti
Serves 6

Ingredients:

225g wholemeal self-raising flour
½ tsp salt
1 tbsp sunflower oil

½ tsp chilli powder
½ tsp cumin
½ tsp tumeric
120ml/ ½ cup hot water

Method:

Sift together the flour and salt. Add the oil to make a soft dough. If you need to add some of the water go ahead. Knead well, cover and leave to rest for about 20-25 minutes.

Split the dough into 6 balls and roll out into think discs.

Heat a little 1- cal spray oil in a pan until nice and hot. Add the roti leave to cook for 30 seconds, flip and do the same on the other side. Cook each one in turn keeping the other warm in the oven.

Roti is another popular Indian bread. Very similar to chapatti it differs only in usually being served slightly thicker. This spicy version takes on a lovely yellow colour from the turmeric.

THE
Skinny INDIAN
TAKEAWAY
RECIPE BOOK

RICE

Rice

No Indian meal is complete without rice. Pilau, Turmeric &
Mushroom rice are three of the most popular dishes.

Pilau Rice
Serves 2

Ingredients:

100g/3 ½ oz basmati rice
½ onion, finely chopped
Handful of shredded cabbage
¼ tsp ground cinnamon
¼ tsp ground cloves

1 bay leaf
Pinch of Saffron
1 chicken stock cube
1 tsp sunflower oil

Method:

Rinse the rice really well in a sieve with cold water.
Boil a pan of water and dissolve a cube of chicken stock into it.
Meanwhile gently fry the onion, cabbage, cinnamon and cloves
for a few minutes. Add the rice to the onion mix and coat, transfer
contents of frying pan plus the bay leaf and saffron into the boiling
stock water and cook until tender.
Drain rice, remove bay leaf, fluff with a fork and serve.

Turmeric Rice
Serves 2

190 CALORIES PER SERVING

Ingredients:

100g/3 ½ oz Basmati Rice
1 spring onion finely chopped
½ tsp turmeric powder
1 bay leaf

Method:

Put the rice in a sieve and rinse well with cold water. Add the rice
to a large pan of salted boiling water along with the turmeric and
bay leaf and cook until tender. Drain, remove the bay leaf and
garnish with the chopped spring onion.

Mushroom Rice
Serves 2

85
CALORIES
PER SERVING

Ingredients:

100g/3½oz basmati rice
100g/3½oz mushrooms finely
50g/2oz frozen peas
½ pepper (any colour is fine)
finely chopped

½ onion, finely chopped
½ tsp garlic powder (or a
crushed garlic clove)
1 bay leaf
Salt to taste

Method:

Rinse the rice really well in a sieve with cold water.
Boil a pan of water. Meanwhile gently fry the onion, pepper,
mushrooms and garlic powder for a few minutes. Add the rice
to the onion and mushroom mix and coat, transfer contents of
frying pan, peas plus the bay leaf and salt into the boiling water
and cook until tender. Drain, remove bay leaf, fluff with a fork and
serve.

THE

Skinny INDIAN
TAKEAWAY
RECIPE BOOK

NOT STRICTLY
TAKEAWAY

A COLLECTION OF RECIPES WHICH, WHILST NOT STRICTLY TAKEAWAY, YOU MIGHT ENJOY TRYING.

Simple Spiced Tomato Soup

Serves 2

175 CALORIES PER SERVING

Ingredients:

1 tsp garam masala
½ tsp cumin
1 tsp ground coriander
½ tsp chilli powder
2 tbsp red lentils
1 x 400g tin chopped tomatoes

1 onion, chopped
500ml/2 cups vegetable stock/broth
Salt & pepper to taste
2 tbsp fat free Greek yoghurt

Method:

Simmer all the ingredients, except the yoghurt, in a saucepan for 15-20 minutes or until the lentils are soft. Tip the contents of the pan into a blender and blend until completely smooth. Top each bowl of soup with a dollop of yoghurt.

Although soup isn't traditionally thought of as a part of a UK takeaway it is an increasingly popular restaurant dish which is super easy to make and low in calories.

Ginger Prawns
Serves 1

Ingredients:

1 onion, chopped
1 tsp sunflower oil
1 tsp turmeric
Salt & pepper to taste
½ tsp garlic powder
½ tsp ginger

½ tsp paprika
½ tsp salt
1 400g/14oz tin chopped tomatoes
200g/7oz raw peeled prawns
2 tbsp fat free Greek yogurt

Method:

Gently sauté the onion in the oil for a few minutes and add the dried spices. Add the chopped tomatoes, simmer for a further 8-10 minutes and add the prawns. Continue to cook for a few minutes until the prawns turn pink and are cooked through. Serve with the yoghurt dolloped on top.

Sometime called Keralan Prawns this dish is a lovely starter when served with a fresh green salad or it can be served with rice and/or bread to make into a main meal.

White Fish & Coconut Curry
Serves 2

Ingredients:

250g/9oz firm white fish fillets
2 portions skinny base mix
1 tsp sunflower oil
1 onion, chopped
1 400g/14oz tin chopped tomatoes

1 tsp garlic powder
½ tsp ground ginger
½ tsp ground coriander
½ tsp salt
Pinch sugar
60ml/ ¼ cup coconut milk

Method:

Gently sauté the onion in the sunflower oil for a few minutes. Add the skinny base mix, chopped tomatoes, dried spices, salt and fish fillets. Cover and leave to gently simmer for aprox 10 minutes, or until the fish is cooked through. Add the coconut milk and warm through for a few minutes. Serve with rice and/or chapattis.

Fish is used widely in Indian cooking. Takeaway fish curry is not hugely popular but it appears tastes are developing and this is a good one to start with. Be careful not to stir the dish too much and break up the fish, you want to keep the fish 'meaty', not too flaky.

Tamarind Potato Salad

Serves 2

Ingredients:

1 tbsp tamarind paste
20g/ ¾ oz sugar (more if needed)
1 tsp ground cumin

1 tsp ground ginger
1 tsp coriander
500g/1lb 2oz salad potatoes
2 tbsp fat free Greek yogurt

Method:

Cook the potatoes in a large pan of salted water for 10 minutes or until the potatoes are tender. Drain and leave to cool. Add all the other ingredients to a pan and gently stir for a few minutes until well combined. Add the potatoes and stir well. Make sure the potatoes are coated well and serve with fat free yoghurt on top.

This authentic Indian dish is lovely served as an extra table dish with friends or side dish to a drier curry.

'Pickled' Indian Greens

Serves 2

88 CALORIES PER SERVING

Ingredients:

1 whole savoy cabbage, shredded
1 tbsp water

1 tsp sugar
3 tbsp white wine vinegar
Pinch salt

Method:

Add the shredded cabbage and water to a pan and cook gently for 5 minutes or until the cabbage is cooked to your liking. Add the sugar, vinegar and salt and cook for a minute or two longer and serve. You may need to alter the balance of sugar, vinegar and salt to get the balance of sweet, sour and salty just right.

This is a simple and quick side dish which is perfect for 'freshening' up any meal. Feel free to use almost any greens you have to hand.

Cauliflower 'Rice'
Serves 2

1 7 0
CALORIES
PER SERVING

Ingredients:

½ large cauliflower head

Method:

Split the cauliflower head into florets and place in a food
processor. Whizz until the cauliflower is the size of rice grains.
Place the 'rice' in a microwavable dish and cook covered for 4-5
minutes or until the 'rice' is piping hot.

*This is a great alternative to rice if you are trying
to keep the calories down. Of course it's not really
rice and it's not really a 'takeaway' but it adds bulk
to a saucy dish if you are watching your weight.
All you need is cauliflower, a food processor and a
microwave. It freezes well too, so make a batch and
freeze into portions.*

Indian Eggs
Serves 2

Ingredients:

3 eggs
1 onion, chopped
1 tsp sunflower oil
2 portions 'skinny' base mix
½ tsp cumin
½ tsp coriander
½ tsp paprika

Pinch salt & sugar
150g/5oz spinach
250g/5oz fresh tomatoes, chopped
120ml/ ½ cup low fat coconut milk

Method:

Hardboil the eggs. Leave to cool then peel and half. Meanwhile gently sauté the onions, spices and tomatoes for a few minutes. Add the spinach and coconut milk; stir and simmer for a few minutes more until the coconut milk is warmed through and the spinach gently wilted. Adjust the seasoning and divide into two bowls place 3 egg halves in each bowl. Lovey served with toasted Indian bread.

This is a great veggie low calories snack curry which can help with curry cravings if you don't want to make a main meal.

THE
Skinny INDIAN
TAKEAWAY
RECIPE BOOK

DRINKS

Mango & Milk
Serves 2

Ingredients:

1 400g/14oz tinned mangoes
250ml/ 1 cup semi skimmed
milk

2 tsp sugar, or more to taste
Handful of ice cubes

Method:

Place all the ingredients in a blender and blend until smooth.
Serve in tall glasses as a dessert or a stand-alone refreshing drink.

*Drinks are considered very important in Indian
cooking. This mango drink can be sweetened to taste
and the use of semi skimmed low fat milk helps with
the calories.*

Strawberry Lassi
Serves 2

110 CALORIES PER SERVING

Ingredients:

400g/14oz strawberries
250ml/1 cup fat free Greek
yoghurt

½ tsp sugar, or to taste
Handful of ice cubes

Method:

Place all the ingredients in a blender and blend until smooth. To
serve pour into glasses with additional ice.

*Lassi is a traditional yogurt based drink from the
Punjab region of which the sweet version is much like
a western smoothie.*

Spiced Lassi
Serves 2

Ingredients:

250ml/1 cup fat free Greek yoghurt
250ml/1 cup water

1 tsp cumin seeds
1 tsp ground coriander

Method:

Whisk the yoghurt and water together until foamy. Add the spices and whisk again until well combined. Garnish with a little chopped fresh coriander if you have it.

This savoury spiced Lassi is often served as a breakfast drink in India.

THE
Skinny INDIAN
TAKEAWAY
RECIPE BOOK

SLOW COOKER
TAKEAWAY

Slow Cooker Anyone?

Another option for super-simple no hassle curry making is to use a slow cooker. It's become a really popular method of cooking and we've responded to readers' requests by including some slow cooker versions of some of the most popular takeaway recipes in this book.

As with the other recipes all the meals serve two, which makes them suitable for cooking in a slow cooker. If you have a large slow cooker, double the ingredients (increase the spices only by 50%) to make sense of the larger cooking surface area.

None of these recipes should take more than 10-15 minutes to prepare. Browning the meat will make a difference to the taste of your recipe but if you really don't have the time, don't worry. It will still taste good.

All meat and vegetables should be cut into even sized pieces. Make sure everything is bite-sized.
All meat should be trimmed of visible fat and the skin removed. The good news is slow cooking is ideal for cheaper meat cuts, any tougher cuts are transformed into meat which melts in your mouth and helps to keep the cost down.

Using Your Slow Cooker: A Few Things

All cooking times are a guide. Make sure you get to know your own slow cooker so that you can adjust things accordingly.

A spray of one cal cooking oil in the cooker before adding ingredients will help with cleaning or you can buy liners.

Be confident with your cooking. Feel free to use substitutes and adjust seasonings/spices to suit your own taste and don't let a missing herb or spice stop you making a meal - you'll almost always be able to find something to replace it.

Bhuna
Serves 2

Ingredients:

2 portions skinny curry base mix
300g/11oz lean meat, cubed
100g/3 ½ oz chopped vegetables
2 onions chopped
¼ tsp cardamom seeds
½ fenugreek seeds and ground ginger

1 tsp ground garlic
1 large tomato chopped
½ red or green pepper sliced
½ tsp each turmeric, chilli powder, ground coriander, cumin & garam masala
1 tbsp low fat natural yoghurt
1 tbsp tomato puree
½ tbsp lemon juice

Method:

Brown the meat in a frying pan with the sunflower oil for a couple of minutes. Add the meat and meat juices to the slow cooker along with all the other ingredients except the yoghurt and lemon juice. Stir well, cover and leave to cook on high for 2-3 hours or low for 4-5 hours or until the meat is tender and cooked through. Stir through the yoghurt and lemon juice just before serving. If you find the curry is a little thick after/during cooking add a few drops of water and stir, alternatively if it is not thick enough after cooking remove the lid and leave to cook on high for 30-40 mins until you get the consistency you require.

Jalfrezi
Serves 2

Ingredients:

2 portions skinny curry base mix
300g/11oz lean meat cubed
1 medium onion thinly sliced
2 tsp sunflower oil
½ tsp each garlic powder, ground ginger, cumin, coriander & turmeric

1 red pepper sliced
1 tsp sugar
½ tsp salt
4 green chillies sliced
1 tsp chilli powder
4 fresh tomatoes, chopped
1 tbsp tomato puree

Method:

Brown the meat in a frying pan with the sunflower oil for a couple of minutes. Add the meat and meat juices to the slow cooker along with all the other ingredients. Stir well, cover and leave to cook on high for 2-3 hours or low for 4-5 hours or until the meat is tender and cooked through. If you find the curry is a little thick after/during cooking add a few drops of water and stir, alternatively if it is not thick enough after cooking remove the lid and leave to cook on high for 30-40 mins until you get the consistency you require.

Korma
Serves 2

359 CALORIES PER SERVING

Ingredients:

2 portions skinny curry base mix
300g/11oz lean meat cubed
1 tsp mild curry powder
¼ tsp ground ginger
½ tsp ground garlic, turmeric, garam masala, cumin
1 bay leaf
60ml/ ¼ cup low fat coconut milk
½ tsp sugar
½ tsp salt
Few drops natural yellow food colouring
2 tsp sunflower oil

Method:

Brown the meat in a frying pan with the sunflower oil for a couple of minutes. Add the meat and meat juices to the slow cooker along with all the other ingredients, except the coconut milk. Stir well, cover and leave to cook on high for 2-3 hours or low for 4-5 hours or until the meat is tender and cooked through. Stir through coconut milk and leave to warm for a few minutes. If you find the curry is a little thick after/during cooking add a few drops of water and stir, alternatively if it is not thick enough after cooking remove the lid and leave to cook on high for 30-40 mins until you get the consistency you require.

Madras
Serves 2

Ingredients:

2 portions skinny curry base mix
300g/11oz Lean meat
2 small onions finely chopped
1 tsp medium curry powder
½ tsp each of turmeric, fenugreek seeds, coriander, garlic powder, ground ginger, paprika & garam masala

3 fresh tomatoes chopped
1 tbsp tomato puree
1 ½ tsp chilli powder
½ tsp crushed cardamom seeds
½ tsp salt
1 tsp sugar
2 tsps lemon juice
2 tsp sunflower oil

Method:

Brown the meat in a frying pan with the sunflower oil for a couple of minutes. Add the meat and meat juices to the slow cooker along with all the other ingredients, except the lemon juice. Stir well, cover and leave to cook on high for 2-3 hours or low for 4-5 hours or until the meat is tender and cooked through. Stir through lemon juice just before serving. If you find the curry is a little thick after/during cooking add a few drops of water and stir, alternatively if it is not thick enough after cooking remove the lid and leave to cook on high for 30-40 mins until you get the consistency you require.

Rogan Josh
Serves 2

399 CALORIES PER SERVING

Ingredients:

2 portions skinny curry base mix
300g/11oz lean cubed meat
1 tsp each garlic powder, ground ginger, cumin powder, garam masala
1 tsp sugar
½ tsp turmeric powder & ground cinnamon

2 tbsp ground almonds
2 tsp curry powder
1 tbsp paprika
½ tsp ground cinnamon
Pinch ground cloves
2 tbsp low fat greek yoghurt
1 tbsp tomato puree
3 chopped tomatoes
½ tsp salt

Method:

Brown the meat in a frying pan with the sunflower oil for a couple of minutes. Add the meat and meat juices to the slow cooker along with all the other ingredients, except the yoghurt. Stir well, cover and leave to cook on high for 2-3 hours or low for 4-5 hours or until the meat is tender and cooked through. Stir through the yoghurt just before serving. If you find the curry is a little thick after/during cooking add a few drops of water and stir, alternatively if it is not thick enough after cooking remove the lid and leave to cook on high for 30-40 mins until you get the consistency you require.

Tikka Masala
Serves 2

Ingredients:

2 portions skinny curry base mix
300g/11oz Tikka Pieces (see page 42 for preparation instructions)
1 tsp sugar
½ tsp salt
1 tsp sunflower oil

½ tsp each of garlic powder, mild chilli powder & ground ginger
1 tsp mild curry powder
2 tbsp tomato puree
3 drops natural red food colouring
2 tbsp low fat greek yoghurt

Method:

Add the tikka pieces (see page 42 for preparation instructions) to the slow cooker along with all the other ingredients, except the yoghurt. Stir well, cover and leave to cook on high for 2-3 hours or low for 4-5 hours or until the meat is tender and cooked through. Stir through yoghurt just before serving. If you find the curry is a little thick after/during cooking add a few drops of water and stir, alternatively if it is not thick enough after cooking remove the lid and leave to cook on high for 30-40 mins until you get the consistency you require.

Vindaloo
Serves 2

380 CALORIES PER SERVING

Ingredients:

2 portions skinny curry base mix
300g/11oz lean meat
2 tsp hot chilli powder (or to your taste)
1 tbsp white wine vinegar
1 tsp turmeric, paprika, garlic, cumin, garam masala

1 onion sliced
1 tbsp tomato puree
1 tsp sugar
½ tsp salt
2 tsp sunflower oil

Method:

Brown the meat in a frying pan with the sunflower oil for a couple of minutes. Add the meat and meat juices to the slow cooker along with all the other ingredients. Stir well, cover and leave to cook on high for 2-3 hours or low for 4-5 hours or until the meat is tender and cooked through. If you find the curry is a little thick after/during cooking add a few drops of water and stir, alternatively if it is not thick enough after cooking remove the lid and leave to cook on high for 30-40 mins until you get the consistency you require.

Conversion Chart

Weights for dry ingredients:

Metric	Imperial
7g	¼ oz
15g	½ oz
20g	¾ oz
25g	1 oz
40g	1½oz
50g	2oz
60g	2½oz
75g	3oz
100g	3½oz
125g	4oz
140g	4½oz
150g	5oz
165g	5½oz
175g	6oz
200g	7oz
225g	8oz
250g	9oz
275g	10oz
300g	11oz
350g	12oz
375g	13oz
400g	14oz
425g	15oz
450g	1lb
500g	1lb 2oz
550g	1¼lb
600g	1lb 5oz
650g	1lb 7oz
675g	1½lb
700g	1lb 9oz
750g	1lb 11oz
800g	1¾lb
900g	2lb
1kg	2¼lb
1.1kg	2½lb
1.25kg	2¾lb
1.35kg	3lb
1.5kg	3lb 6oz
1.8kg	4lb
2kg	4½lb
2.25kg	5lb
2.5kg	5½lb
2.75kg	6lb

Conversion Chart
Liquid measures:

Metric	Imperial	Aus	US
25ml	1fl oz		
60ml	2fl oz	¼ cup	¼ cup
75ml	3fl oz		
100ml	3½fl oz		
120ml	4fl oz	½ cup	½ cup
150ml	5fl oz		
175ml	6fl oz	¾ cup	¾ cup
200ml	7fl oz		
250ml	8fl oz	1 cup	1 cup
300ml	10fl oz/½ pt	1¼ cups	
360ml	12fl oz		
400ml	14fl oz		
450ml	15fl oz	2 cups	2 cups/1 pint
600ml	1 pint	1 pint	2½ cups
750ml	1¼ pint		
900ml	1½ pints		
1 litre	1½ pints	1¾ pints	1 quart

Other CookNation Titles

You may also be interested in other titles in the CookNation series

The Skinny 5:2 Fast Diet Vegetarian Meals For One
Single Serving Fast Day Recipes & Snacks Under 100, 200 & 300 Calories.

The Skinny 5:2 Fast Diet Meals For One
Single Serving Fast Day Recipes & Snacks Under 100, 200 & 300 Calories.

The Skinny 5:2 Bikini Diet Recipe Book
Recipes & Meal Planners Under 100, 200 & 300 Calories. Get Ready For Summer & Lose Weight... FAST!

The Skinny 5:2 Slow Cooker Recipe Book
Skinny Slow Cooker Recipe And Menu Ideas Under 100, 200, 300 & 400 Calories For Your 5:2 Diet.

The Skinny 5:2 Family Favourites Recipe Book
(UK Edition)
Eat With All the Family On Your Diet Fasting Days

The Skinny 5:2 Family Favorites Recipe Book
(USA Edition)
Dine With All The Family On Your Diet Fasting Days

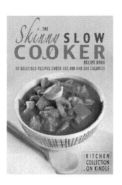

**The Skinny Slow Cooker
Recipe Book**
40 Delicious Recipes Under
300, 400 And 500 Calories.

**The Skinny Paleo Diet Slow
Cooker Recipe Book**
Over 40 Gluten Free Paleo
Diet Recipes For Weight Loss
And Enhanced Well Being.

**The Skinny Slow Cooker
Vegetarian Recipe Book**
40 Delicious Recipes Under
200, 300 And 400 Calories.

**The Healthy Kids
Smoothie Book**
40 Delicious Goodness
In A Glass Recipes for
Happy Kids.

Find all these great titles by searching under
'**CookNation**' on Amazon.

Review
If you enjoyed The Skinny Indian Takeaway Recipe
Book we'd really appreciate your feedback. Reviews
help others decide if this is the right book for them so
a moment of your time would be appreciated. Thank
you.

Printed in Great Britain
by Amazon.co.uk, Ltd.,
Marston Gate.